D0620782

World Leaders

FIDEL CASTRO

rourke biographies

World Leaders

FIDEL CASTRO

by
PAUL MADDEN

Rourke Publications, Inc.
Vero Beach, Florida 32964

Library of Congress Cataloging-in-Publication Data
Madden, Paul, 1940-
  Fidel Castro / written by Paul Madden.
    p.   cm. — (Rourke biographies. World leaders)
  Includes bibliographical references and index.
  Summary: Describes the childhood and rise to power of
Fidel Castro and examines his effect on Cuba.
  ISBN 0-86625-479-X (alk. paper)
  1. Castro, Fidel, 1927-   —Juvenile literature.   2.
Cuba—History—1959-   —Juvenile literature.   3. Heads
of state—Cuba—Biography.   [1. Castro, Fidel, 1927-   .
2. Heads of state.   3. Cuba—History—1959-   ]   I. Title.
II. Series.
F1788.22.C3M33   1993
972.9106′4—dc20   92-46482
                                                          CIP
                                                          AC

Contents

Color Illustrations

World Leaders

FIDEL CASTRO

Chapter 1

Leader or Demagogue?

Huge crowds of people milled about the rundown streets of Havana on the warm and humid morning of January 6, 1959. Their mood seemed festive and excited, yet subdued and expectant. Suddenly a chant became audible over the buzz of private conversations, at first faint and far away, then getting louder as it was repeated by thousands of voices: *FEEdel, FEEdel!* A long column of Jeeps and tanks came rumbling down the street bearing hundreds of bearded men and a few beaming women dressed in army fatigues and toting rifles. All eyes turned to one figure standing erect on the body of a tank.

The physically striking man had a bushy beard from which a huge cigar protruded, and he was dressed as simply as all the others. Fidel Castro had just overthrown a hated dictator, and the multitudes who greeted him in Havana in his moment of triumph were sure that their hero would bring them an age of peace and prosperity.

Castro's critics have called him a demagogue, obsessed with political ideology and blind to the suffering that some of his policies have caused among those very people he wants to help. These charges may, to varying degrees, be true, but there can be little doubt of one thing: Throughout his life, Castro has striven to bring his vision of social justice and a decent standard of living to the people of Cuba. He has also tried to combat what he sees as the exploitation of Third World—the economically destitute people of poor nations—by rich countries such as the United States and some Western European nations. His efforts in both these areas have brought him the admiration of many and the hatred of many more.

Castro and Cuba

Since assuming control of the Cuban state during the revolution of 1956-1959, Castro has overseen a steady rise—almost 20 percent—in the per-capita (per-person) income of his people, according to statistics compiled by American economists and experts on Cuba Hugh S. Thomas, Georges A. Fauriol, and Juan Carlos Weiss.

Just as important, that income is much more evenly distributed among individual Cubans, as is the nation's real wealth (its agricultural land, real estate, and the goods and services that it produces). Before 1960, per-capita income in Cuba was $356, and only 5 percent of the population controlled more than 80 percent of the wealth of the nation. In 1991, per-capita income was well over $1,000 per year, and the wealthiest 5 percent of the population controlled less than 30 percent of the nation's wealth.

Illiteracy, which stood at more than 40 percent in Cuba before Castro's revolution, had virtually disappeared by 1990. Castro and his advisers have made education free and compulsory throughout the nation. Every Cuban may advance as far through the educational system as his or her abilities will allow. Castro's government has also established a health care system that provides adequate medical services to all Cubans without charge. Since the revolution, infant mortality has decreased from 35 to 19 for every 1,000 live births, and life expectancy has increased from 56 to 70 years. Through a comprehensive building program, Castro and his government have provided housing with modern sanitary facilities for a nation in which less than 15 percent of the population had indoor toilets before 1960 and less than 50 percent had running water. Today, almost all Cuban peasants own some land—in stark contrast to 1959, when 8 percent of landowners held 71 percent of the land and more than 60 percent of all peasants were landless.

Castro, surrounded by guards, is mobbed by cheering Cubans on the eve of his victory march on Havana, in 1959. (AP/Wide World Photos)

Castro has also overseen considerable progress in industrialization and modernization in Cuba: paved roads, urban transportation systems, and electricity for rural homes. Despite Castro's diversion of much-needed resources from Cuba to finance his revolutionary activities in other parts of the world, and despite several gross mistakes in economic planning, most Cubans enjoy a higher standard of living today than those who lived before the revolution.

However, these improvements for the Cuban people have come at a high cost. As Castro's many opponents correctly

New leader among his people: Fidel Castro, shortly after the Cuban revolution, explains plans for land reform to farmers in his homeland, Oriente Province. (AP/Wide World Photos)

point out, the citizens of Castro's state do not enjoy many of the human rights guaranteed by democratic governments. In Castro's police state, there is little political or intellectual freedom. Any attempt by Cubans to organize a political movement outside the Communist regime is a criminal offense punishable by imprisonment. In schools and universities, teachers may discuss politics or economics only within the framework of Marxist-Leninist dogma. They may criticize particular government policies or officials, but they may not suggest any alternatives to socialism. Freedom of speech and freedom of the press have virtually disappeared. The only legal newspaper in Cuba today is *Granma*, the official organ of the Cuban Communist Party. Secret police and networks of informants discourage Cuba's citizens from criticizing Castro's government. Many of those who have dared to do so have ended up in prisons or, more often, insane asylums.

Trading personal liberty and basic freedoms for economic progress was probably not necessary. As Castro's opponents point out, other Latin American states have experienced a greater increase in per-capita income than Cuba, without the repression that Castro has imposed on his people. Castro acknowledges this darker side of his regime, but he argues that it is made necessary by the threat to his revolution from the United States. Such oppressive policies, according to Castro, will disappear when the American government ceases its "aggression" toward Cuba.

Castro and the World

Since the revolution, Castro has become a spokesman for Third World nations as well as the dictator of Cuba. His message is that the capitalists of the industrialized nations have systematically exploited the peoples of the rest of the globe for more than two hundred years, destroying their institutions and wasting their natural resources for the benefit of a privileged few. As head of the Cuban state, he has denounced the greed of Western business leaders and has demanded that they use the wealth they have accumulated to help the victims of Western imperialism around the globe. Although this is a very simplistic worldview, it has struck a responsive chord with the poor people of the world.

In order to help Third World nations escape Western domination, Castro has sent large sums of money and troops to aid in "wars of liberation" against Western imperialist nations. In so doing, he has gained the admiration of many people in Africa, Latin America, and Asia. This willingness to use force to achieve his ends has made him a hero in the eyes of some but a villain in the eyes of many others. Unlike India's Mahatma Gandhi or the United States' Martin Luther King, Jr., Castro seems to think that social and economic justice on a world scale cannot be achieved without massive bloodshed.

It is difficult for those who share Castro's high-minded goals to accept this apparent belief that the end justifies the means. Even within Cuba, a new generation of Cubans, born since the revolution, has privately begun to question Castro's use of force and his use of his country's scarce resources to pursue his foreign policy. With the collapse of the Communist Party in the Soviet Union, younger Cubans secretly criticize Castro's dream of world socialism as unattainable. They seem more interested in achieving a higher standard of living for themselves and their families. Many experts on Cuba agree that communism on the island may not outlive the aging dictator himself.

Chapter 2

The Young Rebel

It was several hours before dawn in Oriente Province, the easternmost region of Cuba, on August 13, 1927. The air already steamed with the promise of stifling heat for the coming day. Barely visible in the distance, high mountains presided over dense tropical vegetation. In their palm-roofed huts, wretchedly poor black and Créole families (descendants of the slaves brought to Cuba by the Spanish to work in mines and on plantations) had not yet awakened to begin the hard work of a new day. The huts had no running water, no electricity. Their occupants had no medical care. They could not read or write, and unemployment among them varied from 25 to 50 percent, depending on the farming season. Most of these people were undernourished, sometimes starving.

At 2:00 A.M. in the comfortable house of one of the Oriente's largest landowners, Lina Ruz González gave birth to a twelve-pound boy. She named her son Fidel Alejandro Castro Ruz. He was born on the family farm, Las Manacas, owned by the infant's father, Ángel Castro y Argiz. The farm was located near the small town of Mayarí.

A Self-Made Father

The boy's father, Ángel Castro, had arrived in Cuba during the Spanish-American War (1898) as a cavalry quartermaster in the Spanish army. Born near the city of Lugo in the Celtic Galicia region of northwestern Spain, he settled permanently in Cuba in 1905. Although Cuba was suffering through an economic depression at the time, Castro managed to prosper despite his lack of schooling and job skills. Through several small business enterprises, he made enough money to buy land. Eventually he acquired title to nearly two thousand acres. He used the land to raise sugarcane and cattle, and by the 1950's his net worth exceeded $500,000 (more than $5 million in 1990 dollars). He became politically influential in the area and was able to provide his family with everything they needed. A large and physically imposing man, he believed that the road to success is paved by hard work, strength of character, and a refusal to quit, and he impressed those values—often in a tyrannical manner—on his children.

Ángel Castro's first wife was María Louisa Argota. They had two children, Lidia and Pedro Emilio. The couple was later divorced: Ángel had impregnated one of the maids, Lina Ruz González, the peasant daughter of one of Ángel's friends. Over the next several years, Ángel and Lina lived together out of wedlock and had three children: Ángela, Ramón, and Fidel. Ángel and Lina eventually married and produced four more children: Juana, Raúl, Emma, and Agustina.

In rigidly Catholic Cuba, illegitimacy was a terrible social stigma. Ángel was wealthy and powerful enough to ignore the criticism of his neighbors, but Ángela, Ramón, and Fidel suffered the insults of their peers at home and at school. Fidel became involved in many fistfights over the circumstances of his birth; his illegitimacy would always be a source of great embarrassment.

Childhood on the Farm

Fidel spent his early childhood on the family farm in a comfortable Spanish-style farmhouse. He rode horses and swam with his siblings and friends in the nearby Birán River. Those who knew him at that time would later recall his great energy, which would amaze his colleagues during his years as a revolutionary and then as a head of state. It is also at this time that he became aware of the glaring differences in social

A young, beardless Fidel making a speech in his 1945 high school yearbook photo: politically minded even then. (AP/Wide World Photos)

standing and wealth that marked the people of Oriente Province. He developed a genuine concern for the poor rural masses.

Fidel saw this poverty in stark contrast to the comfort of the foreigners (mostly U.S. citizens) who worked for the United Fruit Company, which owned much of the land in the region and employed many agricultural laborers. For its American employees, the United Fruit Company operated hospitals, schools, swimming pools, and even a country club, as well as stores filled with U.S. goods. Meanwhile, Cuban workers in the region received starvation wages. The foreign employees seemed to flaunt their wealth in the face of the native population. This type of exploitation had been going on since the 1800's, when the United Fruit Company and other American businesses had established themselves in Cuba. These businesses had helped Cuba to market its agricultural products, but mainly to the benefit of the rich. It is no surprise, therefore, that native Cubans—seeing their American neighbors to the north becoming rich by exploiting Cuban resources—came to resent Americans and the wealthy and corrupt Cuban leaders that they supported. Some observers date the beginning of Fidel's antipathy toward the United States to these childhood experiences.

Fidel's father was a very strict parent. Although the Castro children wanted for nothing and were loved by both their parents, conflicts between the authoritarian Ángel and his children occurred regularly. Fidel later described his father as a capitalist who exploited the people who worked for him. Fidel's mother, by contrast, was a deeply religious woman, determined that her children would succeed in life. Unlike his father, Fidel's mother emphasized the importance of education. She had taught herself to read as an adult, and she taught her children that they could achieve anything to which they aspired. Fidel's brother Raúl said years later that the primary reason that Fidel thought education should be available to everyone was his dismay that a woman with the intelligence of his mother had been denied formal schooling.

School in the City

The many accounts of Fidel's early school career contradict one another. Apparently, for the first year or so of his formal schooling, Fidel went to the local school in Birán. In 1933, Fidel's parents decided to send him, Ramón, and Ángela to live with his godparents, Luis Hibbert and his wife Belén Felieú, in Santiago de Cuba. Several of Fidel's biographers have speculated that Ángel and Lina sent the children away to stifle local gossip about their illegitimacy and to spare their children the barbs of their classmates. Castro himself later recalled that his parents decided to send him away because, even at the young age of four, he was a troublemaker at the local school. He also would recall that he was homesick and felt rejected by his parents during his stay with the Hibberts.

In 1935, Fidel's parents enrolled him in a Marist (Catholic) school in Santiago, the La Salle school, as a day student. La Salle's administrators insisted that before any of the Castro children could be enrolled, Ángel and Lina had to take marriage vows and the illegitimate children had to be baptized and confirmed, which was done. Fidel was a year too young to be accepted in the school, so (according to Raúl) his father bribed an official to alter the baptism date on his birth records to read 1926. The official position of the Cuban government today is that Fidel was born in 1926, but his brother Raúl confirms that he was actually born in 1927.

The Castro children were still living with their godparents, but the boys wanted to become boarders at the school, since boarders were able to go on field trips and enjoy other programs. Fidel got his way when he continued to behave badly at home—"a great victory for me," as he later put it.

Fidel excelled in school, both academically and athletically, even though his teachers described him as disruptive because he had many fights with his classmates. According to Raúl, Fidel would never admit defeat. If he were beaten by a boy on one day, he would challenge him again the next day and continue to fight him until he had won.

During his fifth-grade year, the Marist brothers decided that Fidel needed more discipline and transferred him to another Marist school in Santiago, the Dolores school. There, Fidel fought less with his classmates, seeking instead to beat them in the classroom and on the athletic field. However, he still showed the stubborn drive that would be his trademark throughout his life.

In 1942, Fidel persuaded his father to send him to Belén, the famous Jesuit preparatory school in Havana. Wealthy Cubans sent their children to Belén to groom them for university careers. The Jesuit priests who ran the school prided themselves in offering the best education in Cuba and in producing future leaders of the country. Fidel's teachers at Belén permitted freedom of thought, but they also emphasized obedience to authority. They prized intellect and eloquence over materialism. Many of the teachers at Belén were outspoken supporters of Generalissimo Francisco Franco, the Fascist dictator of Spain at that time. Franco represented himself as the champion of Catholicism against the rising threat of communism. During these years, Fidel developed the belief that he was destined for great things—a belief reinforced by his mother and by the Jesuit teachers at the school, who saw that he was an exceptional individual.

Although he received excellent marks in all subjects (largely because of his near-photographic memory), Fidel's favorite subject was Cuban history. He idolized José Martí, a hero of the 1895 Cuban war for independence against Spain and a champion of the poor Cuban masses. Raúl has said that

Fidel tried to speak and write like Martí and was deeply influenced by him throughout his life. Fidel's rural background almost guaranteed that some of the sons of rich city-dwellers at Belén would look down on him. In one of his several attempts to win acceptance at the school, Fidel rode a bicycle full-speed into a brick wall just to prove that he could do things that no one else would even attempt. He also won favor with his peers by excelling in sports.

Fidel had inherited the physical stature of his father. At six feet, three inches in height and weighing more than two hundred pounds, he participated in most sports during his school years, including basketball, baseball, soccer, and jai alai. He was good enough at baseball to try out in 1945 as a pitcher for the Washington Senators of the American League in the United States. By the time Fidel had completed high school, however, he had already decided on a career in politics, leaving no time for professional athletics. In 1945, Fidel was named the outstanding athlete in Cuba for the years 1944-1945. His interest in athletics would continue throughout his life. Even now, he frequently attends the training sessions of Cuban Olympic athletes, who have benefitted from strong state support. That support has allowed Cuban athletes to dominate some Olympic events, such as boxing.

His years in school left Fidel with great admiration for the discipline of the Jesuits and a reverence for what he perceived as true Christianity. He had no use for the formal structure of the Catholic church in Cuba, seeing it as a tool for the wealthy to maintain their privileged positions in society; he believes organized religion to be filled with hypocrisy. Throughout his career, Fidel has displayed conformity to the simple religion taught by his mother, the Christianity that teaches kindness to the poor and unfortunate.

Chapter 3

The Making of a Revolutionary

Fidel Castro matriculated in the School of Law at the University of Havana in September, 1945. He arrived in Havana in a new Ford automobile purchased for him by his father, dressed in a dark blue suit and full of ideals about ways to reform Cuban society. World War II had just ended, and there seemed to be a new tide of freedom in the world, as Third World nations began to seek independence from the formerly dominant countries of Europe, which had been weakened by six years of war. Ramón Grau San Martín was the democratically elected president of Cuba, a man who many Cubans (including Fidel) hoped would at last bring democracy and social reform to his country.

Those who knew Fidel at the time remember him as always being impeccably dressed, full of nervous energy to the point of never being able to relax, and possessing the charisma that marked him as a natural leader. Almost instantly, the aspiring young student found himself caught up in the political turmoil of the university.

University Politics

Castro immediately became involved in the bewildering maze of campus politics at the university. Like Cuban national politics in general, campus politics were marked by frequent episodes of violence. In those days, the line between politics and gangsterism was very thin. Campus politicians hoped to translate student leadership into careers in the national government, and some did not hesitate to threaten their professors into giving good grades, or even murder their rivals, in order to further their ambitions.

When Fidel entered the university, two major political factions, as well as a number of minor groups, competed for political supremacy. Both the major groups tried to recruit Fidel because of his obvious leadership qualities. The largest group was the Unión Insurrecional Revolucionaria (UIR), led by Emilio Tró, a veteran of the Republican army of the Spanish Civil War (1936-1939) and the American army in World War II (1939-1945). Tró's followers espoused nationalism and were vaguely leftist in political orientation. The UIR's main rival on campus was the Movimiento Socialista Revolucionaria (MSR), founded in Castro's freshman year by the fiercely anti-Communist, anti-American Rolando Masferrer. The MSR supported the president of Cuba at that time, Ramón Grau San Martín, who represented himself as a champion of reform and an opponent of corruption in Cuban politics. Grau was the leader of Cuba's largest political party, the *Auténticos*.

Although both political organizations brought heavy pressure on Fidel to join them, he was determined to pursue an independent course, even though such independence was dangerous. Ultimately he managed to alienate the MSR through his constant criticism of the Cuban government and the policies of President Grau. Several MSR members threatened Fidel's life, and an official of the national government itself told him to cease criticizing the government or leave the campus forever. Fidel refused to be intimidated and continued both his studies and his anti-government political agitation. To protect himself, he became closely associated with the UIR, but he never actually joined it. Fidel's classmates elected him freshman class representative to the law school, where he received excellent grades in his studies.

During his second year at the university, Fidel's classmates again elected him as their representative. He and a number of other independent students on campus began to associate themselves with the political program of Eduardo ("Eddy") Chibás, a populist member of the *Auténtico* party with a weekly radio show. Cubans loved Chibás, almost as much as they loved their legendary hero José Martí. During the 1930's, Chibás had fought against the corrupt dictator Gerardo

Outside the presidential palace in Havana, 1933: students demonstrate against Fulgencio Batista, then the leader of Cuba's armed forces and later the corrupt president whom Castro would overthrow. (AP/Wide World Photos)

Machado, and now Chibás was a senator. On the radio, Chibás denounced the corruption in Cuban politics and frequently exposed some of the most corrupt members of the government.

In May of 1947, Chibás broke away from the *Auténticos* to form a new political party, the Cuban People's Party (PPC), popularly known as the *Ortodoxos*. Castro was the only student leader asked to attend the meeting at which the new party was established. The platform of the *Ortodoxos* emphasized anti-imperialism, economic independence, political liberty, social justice, and a vaguely defined socialism. Because these were exactly the principles Castro associated with Martí and which he himself espoused, he joined the new party and remained a leading member for eight years. Joining the new party marked the beginning of Castro's involvement in politics at the national—not just the university—level.

While Castro was heavily engaged in his studies and in trying to organize the new party on campus, several unexpected occurrences changed the course of his career. The first was an ill-fated revolutionary adventure in the Dominican Republic, which marked the beginning of Castro's concern for social justice in areas other than Cuba. The second was a symbolic robbery that Castro arranged to call attention to government corruption and to rally support for change. Finally, Castro attended a Pan-American student conference in Bogotá, Colombia. Taken together, these events launched Castro onto both the national and the international political stage.

An Aborted Overthrow

In 1930, General Rafael Trujillo had seized power in the Dominican Republic, the nation that occupied the western two-thirds of Hispaniola (the big island immediately southwest of Cuba). For more than fifteen years, Trujillo suppressed any opposition to his rule, murdering his enemies and enriching himself and his friends at the expense of the wretchedly poor Dominican people.

One of the leaders of the MSR, Manolo Castro (no relation to Fidel), organized an armed force of twelve hundred men, including Cuban idealists, Dominican exiles, and soldiers of fortune, to overthrow Trujillo. The plan initially had the support of the Grau government, in part to gain the support of the large and influential Dominican exile community in Cuba.

By this time, Fidel's political activities had angered the MSR and the Grau government, which would have been happy to see him killed. Fidel agreed to participate in the overthrow of Trujillo, but only when he was assured by Manolo Castro that he would not be killed by MSR leader Rolando Masferrer. Fidel and the other men were sent to Oriente Province, near his home, for military training; then they trained on the small island of Cayo Confites. In the meantime, Trujillo had heard of the expedition and appealed to President Harry Truman of the United States, who in turn demanded that Grau disband the expedition.

Suddenly—apparently bowing to this pressure from the U.S. government—President Grau sent the Cuban navy to intercept the small fleet of MSR boats before they reached the Dominican Republic. Fidel managed to escape arrest by jumping overboard and swimming to land through waters heavily infested with sharks. The episode demonstrates some typical Castro traits: not only his fearlessness but also his determination never to be stopped or defeated.

A Bell for Cuba

Returning to the university from the Cayo Confites expedition, Castro again became heavily involved in *Ortodoxo* politics on campus. His activities almost resulted in his arrest by agents of President Grau. With new elections scheduled for the following year, Cuban politics became increasingly violent.

Murders became an almost daily occurrence. One of the casualties was a student, Carlos Martínez. His death angered the entire student population at the University of Havana and gave Fidel a cause to propel him to greater prominence in the student community.

Fidel helped organize a nationwide student strike to protest the corruption of the Grau administration. During the student rallies, Fidel realized that he had the power to motivate huge crowds with his passionate speeches. According to documents of the Grau government, released after Castro came into power, government agents tried to assassinate Fidel on several occasions during this time. A born politician with a flair for drama, Fidel concocted a symbolic gesture to focus even more attention on himself.

In the village of Manzanillo in Fidel's native Oriente Province rested the historic bell of Demajagua. Rebels in Cuba's 1868 attempt to overthrow Spanish rule had rung the bell to signal the start of their revolution, and it had become a famous symbol of freedom. Fidel decided to bring the bell to Havana. There, its ringing would rally the people to march on the presidential palace, where they would demand Grau's resignation. Fidel persuaded Manzanillo's mayor to take the three-hundred-pound bell to Havana by train, where friends helped him load it into a convertible. They proceeded triumphantly to the rector's office at the university.

During the night, as Castro and his student supporters planned their march on the presidential palace, agents of Grau stole the bell. A huge student rally convened the next night, but the bell was not there. Nevertheless, Fidel gave what his admirers thought was the best speech of his career to that time. Castro emotionally criticized Grau for having "betrayed the revolution and delivering the nation's wealth to foreigners." Castro had already learned the enormous appeal such charges had for the Cuban people. He also accused Grau of increasing the level of government corruption, rather than ending it as he had promised.

Grau eventually returned the bell to Manzanillo. The episode attracted much attention to Fidel and marked him as a man of destiny. In the eyes of Grau, however, Fidel was a troublesome nuisance to be eliminated.

The Pan-American Conference

In part to avoid the Cuban police, Castro embarked in March, 1948, for Bogotá, Colombia, to participate in an international student congress sponsored by Argentine president Juan Perón. On the way to the congress, Castro met with student leaders in Panama, the Dominican Republic, and Venezuela, where he learned that his own anti-imperialism and anti-Americanism were passionately shared by many students throughout Latin America.

During the conference, the murder of one of the speakers provoked a citywide riot that almost turned into a revolution. Fidel, according to his own later account, joined the revolutionaries. With a surging crowd of students, he invaded a police station, where he armed himself with a teargas gun and several rounds of ammunition. He also took a military cape, a cap, and a pair of boots. Later he managed to acquire a pistol and sixteen bullets. The mob, of which he was now part, moved on to the presidential palace, where soldiers fired on the crowd. A night of violence followed. Fidel, horrified, realized that this was not truly a revolution but only anarchy.

He came away from the experience convinced that social change should come not through bloody revolution but through reform led by charismatic leaders with overwhelming public support. When he returned to the University of Havana, Castro abandoned campus politics and concentrated his political efforts on building the *Ortodoxos* into a party of national reform and establishing himself as one of its leaders.

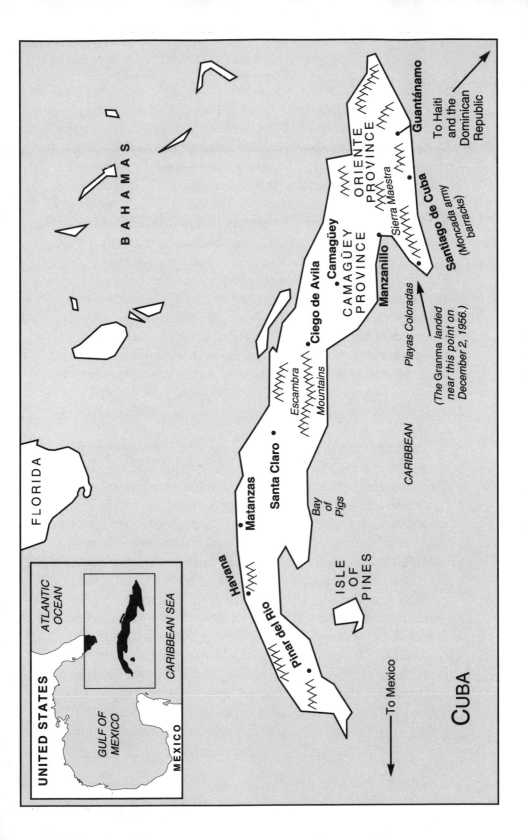

From Orthodox Politician to Revolutionary

On October 12, 1948, Fidel married Mirta Díaz-Balart, the sister of one of his classmates; he had known her for only a few months. Mirta, who was studying philosophy at the university, came from a well-to-do family in Oriente Province, the members of which actively disliked Fidel. The young couple spent their honeymoon in the United States, where Fidel acquired a copy of Karl Marx's *Das Kapital*—probably his first exposure to pure Marxism. Then they returned to Havana, where they settled in a one-room hotel flat and continued their studies. By many reports, Mirta was the only woman Fidel ever loved. She bore his only legitimate child, Fidelito, on September 14, 1949. For some time after the wedding, Fidel reduced his political activities and concentrated on his studies. During his final year at the university, he met and became friends with several members of the Cuban Communist Party, but he remained loyal to Chibás and the *Ortodoxos*.

Castro graduated during the summer of 1950 with three doctorates: in law, social sciences, and diplomatic law. He had spent relatively little time during his university career studying; instead, politics had taken up most of his time. When it came time for final examinations, he managed to cram four years of study into a few weeks, thanks to his incredible memory. After graduation, he left the university intent on making a career in politics and law.

Fidel and Mirta settled into what promised to be a successful, if ordinary, life. They moved into a tiny apartment in Havana, where Fidel opened a law practice with two of his classmates. The young couple was always short of money, even though Fidel's father still extended an allowance to him for domestic support. Fidel cared little for paying his own bills. Once, the couple's rented furniture was repossessed by the owner. Yet he would immediately give money to any friend or client who needed it. In return, many of the poor Cubans whom he helped were quick to give him free food or do favors for him.

Fidel continued to harbor political ambitions and to work on behalf of Chibás and the *Ortodoxos*. Chibás planned to run for president of Cuba in 1952, and Fidel campaigned hard for his hero. In August, however, Chibás, humiliated because several people had accused him of lying during his radio program, shot himself in the stomach during a broadcast. Fidel, who was with Chibás when the incident occurred, maintained a constant vigil at his hospital bedside until his hero died. The *Ortodoxos* were left without a leader.

After Chibás' death, Fidel decided to offer himself as an *Ortodoxo* candidate for the Cuban parliament. Chibás' successors did not endorse the young lawyer. They feared that he would oust them as leaders of the *Ortodoxo* party, and in fact Castro had made no secret of his belief that, with Chibás dead, the mantle of leadership should rightly fall to him. Undeterred by his failure to gain the endorsement of his party, Fidel pursued his campaign independently. He began exposing government corruption: both on the radio, as Chibás had done, and in the columns of *Alerta*, a liberal newspaper. There is every reason to believe that Castro would have won a seat in parliament had the election been held as scheduled. Instead, the election did not take place, thanks to the actions of Fulgencio Batista.

Chapter 4

Corruption in Cuba

Fulgencio Batista had been powerful in Cuba for many years. Usually content to let others occupy the office of president of Cuba while he actually controlled the government through his command of the army, Batista had finally taken over the top political office of Cuba in 1940. He retired into private life in 1944, only to re-emerge as a candidate in 1952. Thinking one of his opponents had rigged the upcoming election, he decided to elect himself. Batista seized the presidency and began an era of corrupt government that equaled or exceeded the abuses of power that Cuba had seen in the past. Without intending to do so, he also ignited a revolutionary fervor that would result in Castro's revolution four years later.

Many observers of Cuban politics have pointed out that Cuba, with or without Fidel Castro, was ripe for revolution in the 1950's for a number of reasons. Most of these reasons arose from a long history of repression, beginning in the 1800's and continuing into the 1950's. To understand why Fidel had such a powerful influence on the Cuban people, and to understand Fidel himself, it is necessary to know something about the history of Cuba.

The Cuban Dilemma

The people of Cuba have been dominated by other nations since the Spanish conquered the island in the 1500's. Many times they have revolted against their conquerors, usually without success and often with great loss of life. From the revolt led by the revolutionary hero José Martí, in 1895, to

President Fulgencio Batista, toting a pistol, celebrates shortly after his coup d'état *in 1952.* (AP/Wide World Photos)

Castro's revolution of 1956-1959, the Cuban people have continuously had their hopes for true independence raised and then dashed as idealistic leaders have been forced to serve the interests of the businesses or governments of foreign lands. Even Castro's revolution has not been able to escape this foreign influence completely.

Early Revolution .

The first large-scale revolt against Spanish rule in Cuba occurred in 1868. Almost all sectors of Cuban society, including business people, farmers, and slaves, participated in the attempt to overthrow Spanish rule in Cuba, free the slaves, and establish a democratic government.

The war lasted for ten years, until 1878. Soldiers on both sides fought with great courage and ruthlessness. Many acts of cruelty were committed by both the rebels and the Spanish government authorities, making each side very bitter toward the other. Twice during the struggle, the leaders of the Cuban rebels asked representatives of the U.S. government to annex the island so that the American army could provide protection, but many people in the United States objected to annexation, and it never came about.

The war lasted so long only because there was a power struggle going on in Spain which prevented the Spanish government from dealing with Cuba. The power struggle was finally resolved when Alfonso XII took the throne in 1874. The Spanish sent a large military force to Cuba in 1878; it defeated the rebel army by May of that year. Authoritarian Spanish rule was restored on the island, but many of the rebels fled abroad (especially to the United States) and began to plan for a new uprising. One positive result of the revolution was the emancipation of Cuban slaves in 1879, but the emancipation did not go into effect until 1888.

Although there were a few uprisings against Spanish rule

during the years 1878-1895, they were easily suppressed by the Spanish. The next major independence movement, however, would live long in the minds of future Cubans.

José Martí and Cuban Independence

Born in Havana to Spanish parents, José Martí (1853-1895) was an ardent champion of Cuban independence during the war of 1878, although he did not participate in the fighting. As early as 1879, he began to conspire with young Cubans at home and abroad in a new attempt to end Spanish rule over his homeland. In 1890, he founded *La Liga de Instrucción* (the League of Instruction) in New York City. This was a sort of training school for revolutionaries. Martí's command of foreign languages led to his appointment as head of the Argentine and Paraguayan consuls in the United States. In these positions, he was able to meet many influential American citizens, who became sympathetic to his cause. He persuaded many native Cuban workers in the United States (especially those working in Florida) to contribute one-tenth of their earnings to his Cuban Revolutionary Party.

Martí was as fearful of U.S. domination as he was of continued Spanish rule. He had good reason for his fear of the United States, because many prominent Americans (including future president Theodore Roosevelt) were openly advocating U.S. acquisition of colonies abroad.

Martí launched his revolution during a world economic depression in 1895. Almost from the beginning, the revolution received great publicity from the U.S. newspapers owned by William Randolph Hearst. Hearst and many of his wealthy friends hoped that the United States would annex Cuba, and they saw Martí's revolution as a means to their own end. Hearst's newspapers immediately began publishing a series of often dishonest stories about the corruptness of Spanish administration in Cuba, the justice of Martí's cause, and the cruel acts committed by Spanish troops against Cuban civilians. The Spanish killed Martí in one of the first skirmishes of the war. His fame as a martyr to Cuban freedom and independence grew, and today he is revered as Cuba's greatest national hero.

The war went badly for the remaining rebels until the U.S. government, pushed by the supposed "public opinion" represented by Hearst's newspapers, intervened in 1898. The U.S. Army and Navy quickly defeated the Spanish both in the Philippine Islands and in Cuba. In the peace treaty, the American government forced the Spanish to give much of their overseas empire to the United States and to grant Cuba its independence.

The Platt Amendment

In the immediate aftermath of the Spanish surrender, American military officers became the governors of the different provinces of Cuba. These military governments stayed in power until 1902. To the disgust of many Cuban revolutionaries, they often kept the old Spanish civil authorities in power. Despite the demands in the Hearst newspapers that the United States annex Cuba, U.S. government officials decided against it. During the period of U.S. military occupation, many American individuals and companies made large investments in Cuban land and began building industrial plants on the island.

In 1901, the United States Congress adopted the Platt Amendment, which placed Cuban foreign policy under the control of the United States and gave the U.S. military the right to intervene in Cuban affairs to "preserve Cuban independence and [maintain] stable government" whenever the United States thought it necessary. Many Cubans bitterly resented the Platt Amendment and hated the United States because of it. The amendment would not be repealed until 1934.

The first elections for an independent parliament were held in 1904, and the first election of a president was held in 1905. During the presidential campaign, gangster-like political factions used intimidation and murder to sway the vote; these tactics would continue to characterize Cuban politics. After the election, President Theodore Roosevelt used the Platt Amendment to allow him to send two thousand U.S. Marines to Cuba to "preserve order." Actually, he wanted to protect the property and interests of U.S. businesses from the gangsters, whom the Cuban government could not control. This renewed U.S. military "government" remained in power in Cuba until 1909.

More Foreign Exploitation

From 1909 until 1934, a series of Cuban governments, dominated by the United States, seemed more interested in lining their pockets with the money of Cuba's citizens than in working toward good government. Corruption was the rule rather than the exception, driving the already poor population into deeper poverty. Wealthy officials and business owners lived lives of luxury in the cities, while the population in the countryside grew more desperate.

In 1933, widespread strikes against the U.S.-controlled government of General Gerardo Machado (1871-1939) signaled that the era of U.S. domination of Cuba might be ending. When it became clear that there would be a full-scale revolution if Machado remained in power, he resigned at the insistence of the U.S. government. However, the U.S.-backed regime that replaced Machado was no more popular with the Cuban people than Machado's government had been.

In September, 1933, some officers of the Cuban army, led by Sergeant Pablo Rodríguez, overthrew the government. Rodríguez soon lost his leadership of the revolt to Fulgencio Batista.

Two weeks after coming to power, Castro criticizes the U.S. support of the overthrown Batista regime as a reporter takes notes. (AP/Wide World Photos)

Batista: The Last Straw

Batista, who had joined the army as a private in 1921, was a powerful figure in Cuban politics after 1933. He served as president from 1940 to 1944. Always a force to be reckoned with in Cuban politics, he was usually the power behind the various civilian governments.

Like other Cuban leaders, Batista had been corrupted by foreign money. In 1952, he was again a candidate for the presidency. He used the issues of graft and corruption and a mounting hysteria over Communist activities in Cuba to justify seizing power and ousting the regime of President Carlos Prío Socarrás. Batista then canceled the upcoming elections in order to "preserve order."

Batista's actions destroyed Castro's orthodox political career before it had begun. In retrospect, the Batista *coup d'état* (overthrow of the government) was an important turning point—not only in Castro's career but also in the course of world history. Denied a position in democratic politics, Castro abandoned his earlier conviction that social change should be made peacefully. He now decided to become a revolutionary. After Batista's seizure of power, Castro concentrated all his efforts on overthrowing Batista and bringing social justice to the Cuban people.

The regime installed by Batista in 1952 was as corrupt as its predecessors. Batista and his friends looted the country, lining their own pockets with tax money and taking bribes from the Mafia and similar organizations to allow them to operate gambling casinos, prostitution rings, and narcotics enterprises. Batista's government also took graft in exchange for granting U.S. companies monopolies in Cuba, charging very little in taxes. In addition, Batista and his friends suppressed any opposition to their activities and any open criticism of their government. Batista and his supporters lived in luxury while the huge majority of the Cuban people lived in the worst poverty. As a result, Batista became extremely unpopular with most Cubans.

Ripe for Revolt

By the 1950's, three groups were intent on making major changes in Cuban society through revolution: the liberal revolutionaries, the nationalists, and the Communists.

The liberal revolutionaries came largely from the Cuban middle class and included doctors, lawyers, college professors, and business people. They made up the membership of several organizations that advocated more or less the same program: free and open elections, an economic policy that would favor native Cuban businesses and would accelerate industrialization, a bill of rights like that of the United States to guarantee and protect civil liberties, and an end to corruption in government.

The nationalists came largely from the Cuban business community. They shared many of the goals of the liberals but believed that the most important goal for any Cuban government was the elimination of foreign domination of the Cuban economy and the Cuban government. The members of this group were critical of the United States and its business community. They felt that America held Cuba as a colony, just as European nations still held many areas of the Third World.

The final group, the Communists, did not have a large following among the Cuban people. The Cuban Communist Party drew its members from intellectuals disgusted by Cuba's history of political corruption and convinced that only a socialist dictatorship could free Cuba from the grip of imperialism. The Party's leaders took orders directly from Joseph Stalin and the Russian Communist Party.

Most of the members of these three groups could agree on at least two points: first, that the Batista regime was evil and must be destroyed; and second, that the United States and its business community exercised far too much control of the Cuban government and economy, and that control should be curtailed.

Many students of revolutions argue that a revolution cannot occur unless a charismatic leader emerges to move the people to successful revolt. Both critics and supporters of Fidel Castro acknowledge that he possessed the charisma—the ability to motivate his people—and he used that ability to place himself at the head of the various Cuban revolutionary groups.

Chapter 5

Road to Revolution

Immediately after the Batista *coup*, Castro wrote a pamphlet denouncing Batista as a tyrant and calling on young Cubans to be prepared to sacrifice their lives in a fight for freedom. Some of Castro's friends mimeographed the pamphlet and distributed it throughout Havana. Many of Castro's friends within the *Ortodoxo* party began to conspire with him to overthrow Batista. Castro also became the political editor for the underground newspaper *El Acusador* (*The Accuser*). He wrote articles in which he violently denounced the Batista government and encouraged armed rebellion. Castro signed these articles with his middle name, Alejandro, which became his revolutionary name for many years—some say because it reminded him of Alexander the Great.

During the summer of 1952, Castro began to turn his network of friends into a revolutionary movement. In several cities and villages, Castro's friends organized military training units, each composed of ten revolutionaries and their leader. The leaders answered directly to Castro. Almost all of those who joined this young military force were between the ages of eighteen and twenty-two. Secrecy characterized Castro's organization, Fidel keeping to himself his ultimate plans for the group he had organized. During this period he established contacts with other revolutionary leaders throughout Cuba.

Moncada: Birth of a Movement

By February, 1953, Castro and Abel Santamaría (his chief lieutenant at the time) decided to use their fledgling military force to seize a military installation. They reasoned that, if they were successful, their actions would spark a general uprising against the Batista regime. The two men were inspired by several failed uprisings against Batista by other groups during the winter of 1952-1953, and by a meeting in Montreal attended by leaders from all the various revolutionary groups.

Santamaría and Castro hand-picked 150 of their followers to seize the Moncada military barracks located at Santiago de Cuba, in Castro's home province of Oriente. The revolutionaries included Fidel's younger brother Raúl, who had already become one of his brother's most loyal supporters. Castro told his wife Mirta nothing of the adventure.

Castro launched his ill-fated attack in the early-morning hours of July 26, 1953. At 5:00 A.M. he left the motel in Moncada, where he had assembled his forces at the head of a convoy of twenty-six automobiles. Before their departure, Fidel made a brief speech to his men. He was eloquent and inspiring, as usual, but several of his followers later recalled that he seemed to expect that the attack would fail—as though he were seeking martyrs and even death for himself.

Arriving at the gate to the barracks, three men in the lead car jumped out and yelled at the guards, "Attention! The general is coming!" Fidel's men were dressed in army fatigues, which fooled the guards long enough for the rebels to disarm them, take the chain from across the gate to the barracks, and allow Fidel's convoy to pass. Before all of the automobiles could pass through the gate, they were discovered by a roving patrol. Both sides began shooting.

Meanwhile, another group of rebels, led by Lester Rodríguez and Raúl, successfully stormed the Palace of Justice across the street and began to provide covering fire for Fidel's group. On the opposite side of the barracks, a third column of rebels, commanded by Santamaría, captured the Saturnino Lora Civil Hospital. All the rebels except Fidel's men had secured their objectives.

Braving heavy fire, Fidel led about fifty of his fighters into the barracks. They were unable to locate their two main objectives, the weapons and the radio equipment. These had been moved the day before to make room for a military band that was scheduled to play for a festival. By 6:00 A.M., the soldiers were fully awake, and Fidel and his men were in danger of being captured. Fidel gave the order to retreat.

Despite the bravery of Fidel and his men, their actions were unsuccessful, and most of them were either killed or eventually captured and put on trial for armed insurrection (revolt). The trial of Castro and his fellow insurrectionists, which began on September 21, 1953, immediately gained national attention. Castro was given a separate trial on October 16, at which he gave an emotional and eloquent two-hour speech denouncing tyrants such as Batista and claiming that the rebels' cause would one day be triumphant. The media coverage of this trial was censored, but Marta Rojas, a young journalist at the time and later the editor of the Cuban government's official newspaper *Granma*, transcribed Castro's closing statement, which would become famous to all Cubans:

> . . . I know that jail will be as hard as it has ever been . . . ; but I do not fear this, as I do not fear the fury of the miserable tyrant who snuffed out the life of seventy brothers of mine. Condemn me, it does not matter. *History will absolve me!*

The entire statement, reproduced in several forms and distributed widely throughout Cuba, became the most important summary of the goals of Castro's revolution, and the base on which his July 26 Movement grew.

Imprisoned on the Isle of Pines

Despite his eloquent defense, Castro and his brother Raúl, along with most of the other defendants, were convicted and sentenced to various terms of imprisonment. Prison officials then transported the convicted men to the Isle of Pines, off the southwestern coast of Cuba, where they remained until May 15, 1955. While in prison, Castro read much of the great literature of the world, as well as the works of such great political philosophers as John Locke, Thomas Jefferson, and Vladimir Ilich Lenin. To Fidel's dismay, Mirta divorced him during his prison term. The couple had grown increasingly distant as a result of Castro's seeming lack of concern for his family's material welfare and his obsession with the demands of politics.

His friends and followers in Cuba used the time to enlarge Castro's organization and widely distribute *History Will Absolve Me* (sometimes called the Moncada Manifesto). Castro, who before the the Moncada attack was still relatively unknown among the masses of the Cuban people, became a nationally recognized figure, and his July 26 Movement became one of the most important parts of Cuba's still-fractured surge toward revolution.

Exile in Mexico

On May 7, 1955, Batista felt secure enough to grant general *amnesty* (or pardon) to all political prisoners. Castro and his followers returned to Havana a few days later, still intent on overthrowing the government by force of arms. Castro immediately began to enlarge the organization built by his supporters during his imprisonment. Using *History Will Absolve Me* as their platform, Castro and his friends established a secret network of revolutionaries in the cities and countryside throughout Cuba. Castro continued to denounce the Batista government in newspaper columns and on the radio. He also established dictatorial control of all the activities of his movement.

As his organization grew, Castro began to fear that he would be imprisoned again by the government. He decided to

go into voluntary exile in Mexico, from where he would direct
the activities of his followers in Cuba. On July 7, 1955, Castro
left for Mexico City.

In Mexico, Castro established contact with other Cuban
exiles opposed to Batista and began planning his return to
Cuba at the head of an armed force. One individual who joined
Fidel in Mexico and became important to his success was
Camilo Cienfuegos. Another was a young Argentine physician
named Ernesto Guevara Lynch, who later became famous as
"Che" Guevara.

Guevara, like Castro, was an idealist who blamed Western
imperialism for most of the problems of the world. Also like
Castro, he was willing to use any means necessary to destroy a
corrupt government and to advance his notions of social and
economic justice. Guevara enlisted in Castro's cause, and
together the two men developed a plan to overthrow Batista in
Cuba. Guevara helped Castro establish friendly relationships
with members of the Mexican government, who initially
ignored Castro as he organized and trained an armed group of
men to invade Cuba.

The Voyage of the *Granma*

After more than a year, Guevara and Castro evolved a plan
that they were sure would result in Batista's overthrow. They
would return to Cuba at the head of a group of armed followers
and establish themselves in the mountains of Castro's native
Oriente Province. There they could hide from Batista's soldiers
and slowly establish control of first the province and
eventually all Cuba as the population in the countryside rallied
to their cause.

On the night of November 24, 1956, Castro, Guevara, and
eighty followers embarked for Cuba, packed aboard an aging
yacht named *Granma*, which had been purchased with funds
provided by former president Carlos Prío Socarrás. On

1. Fidel delivers one of his many fiery speeches. (AP/Wide World Photos)

2. Havana as seen from Morro Castle, built between 1589 and 1610 to protect the entrance to the harbor. (Karpan Photo)

3. Fidel Castro, a few years after the revolution. (AP/Wide World Photos)

4. An official portrait. (AP/Wide World Photos)

5. Agricultural workers harvesting bananas in El Paraiso, Cuba. (Lou DeMatteis)

6. Shoppers wait in line at a bakery in Havana. (Lou DeMatteis)

7. Members of the Pioneers, a children's revolutionary organization, attend a political
   rally in Havana. (Karpan Photo)

8. Varadero, Cuba: The sign reads, "Fidel, we will be victorious." (Lou DeMatteis)

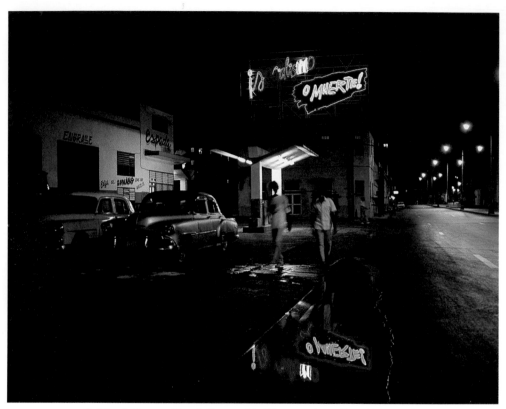

9. "Socialism or Death," says this Havana sign. (Lou DeMatteis)

10. A street in Trinidad, one of Cuba's most historic cities. (Karpan Photo)

11. Today's Cuban economy benefits from tourism supported by luxury hotels such as the Panta Arena, in Varadero. (Karpan Photos)

12. Castro, in 1989, tells a crowd in Camaguey, Cuba, of social and economic advances since the revolution. (AP/Wide World Photos)

13. Castro speaks to participants at a rally in Havana in 1990—still popular with many of Cuba's citizens. (AP/Wide World Photos)

14. The veteran revolutionary waves to his people. (AP/Wide World Photos)

December 2, after a storm-tossed crossing of the Gulf of
Mexico (during which most of them became seasick), they
landed—or, more accurately, they were wrecked—on the
southwestern coast of Oriente Province, near the small city of
Belic. The group lost most of its heavy weapons in the stormy
seas and left the rest aboard the *Granma* as they waded ashore.

*Fidel (with sunglasses), Che (seated, second from left), and twenty fellow revolu-
tionaries shortly after being arrested in Mexico City for plotting the assassination
of Cuban president Fulgencio Batista in June, 1956.* (AP/Wide World Photos)

Batista's soldiers almost immediately spotted Fidel's band
and opened fire on them. Fidel and his men fled toward the
mountains with more than a thousand soldiers in pursuit. On
the second day of their flight, after not having eaten anything
since before the landing, the rebels came to a sugarcane field,
where they chewed the raw cane to gain energy. Extremely
tired and with blistered feet because their boots fit poorly, the
men marched at night and slept under cover during the day. On
December 5, 1956, while they were hiding in a wooded area
near yet more sugarcane fields, they were ambushed by a
government patrol. Thirty-nine men were captured; eighteen of

them were executed without trial. Three more were killed, and only Fidel and twenty comrades, several of whom were wounded, managed to escape. The small band made it to a prearranged assembly point, the small farm of Ramón Pérez, on December 16. Over the following eight days, a few more survivors made their way to Pérez's farm, including Raúl and Che.

Even though their situation looked hopeless, Fidel exuded confidence. "Now we are going to win," he told his comrades. Fidel and the slowly growing group of supporters retreated into the mountains and began to pursue the plan that they had evolved in Mexico. Cuba and the world would never again be the same.

The Guerrilla War

Only Castro and eighteen men from the *Granma* managed to escape being killed or captured by Batista's army and make their way to the Sierra Maestra mountains in Oriente Province. Slowly the rebels gained the confidence of the people of the province and recruits for Castro's band began finding their way to his camp in the mountains. One of the volunteers, Celia Sánchez, became Castro's most trusted aide. She was indispensable to the ultimate success of the revolution, taking responsibility for all the guerrillas' daily needs, including food and ammunition. Celia also began to coordinate the activities of Fidel's men with those of other revolutionary groups in Cuba and acted as a liaison between him and all the leaders of other movements opposed to Batista's government.

Castro's men began attacking government military outposts throughout Oriente Province, with great success. In his dealings with the poor peasants of the region, Castro always paid farmers for any produce his troops took and promised land reform. These activities gained widespread attention in Cuba and in the United States through articles written by

Herbert L. Matthews, a senior editor of *The New York Times*.

Castro granted Matthews an exclusive interview in February, 1957. During the interview, Castro convinced the journalist that his guerrillas were much more numerous and his movement much more widespread than was actually the case. Matthews' first article about Castro appeared in the *Times* on February 24, 1957. The story described Fidel as a combination of Robin Hood and Thomas Jefferson. Despite Batista's denials that Castro was even alive (much less leading a large revolutionary army), the story eventually became available to the Cuban people. Castro's name became known throughout the United States and was associated with democratic revolution against a corrupt dictatorship. In Cuba, Matthews' articles made Castro an instant national hero.

The notoriety Castro gained through the press brought his July 26 Movement large numbers of new recruits in 1957 and 1958, including intellectuals and members of the middle class in the cities of Cuba. The leaders of other revolutionary groups and the traditional political parties in Cuba began looking to Castro as the leading figure of the revolution and coordinated their efforts with his.

As anti-government activity accelerated in Cuba, Batista reacted with even more repressive policies. The mounting repression alienated more and more Cubans from Batista's regime and drove them into the ranks of the revolutionaries, especially the July 26 Movement. Even some of the noncommissioned officers in Batista's army secretly joined Castro's movement after a well-publicized victory for Castro's forces at the military outpost at El Uvero. Fidel personally commanded the successful attack on the installation, which made Batista react with even more repression. Batista's brutality, however, had the effect of turning international opinion against him and creating worldwide sympathy for Castro and his guerrillas.

By the beginning of 1958, Batista's regime was tottering on the brink of collapse. Guerrillas led by Castro pushed down from the mountains and established permanent bases in the lowlands. In the cities, members of the July 26 Movement began planning a *general strike* (a work-stoppage by all workers in all industries in Cuba) to cripple the nation's economy. Castro and other leaders hoped that the general strike, coordinated with the guerrilla military activity, would

Castro's militia during a revolutionary battle near Treasure Lagoon, southeast of Havana. (AP/Wide World Photos)

68

topple Batista and his supporters.

The general strike took place in April, 1958, but failed as a result of poor planning. Emboldened by the seeming disarray of his enemies, Batista launched a major military offensive against Castro's guerrillas in May. Despite overwhelming superiority in numbers, Batista's hired troops proved no match for Castro's followers, who were fighting for an ideal. By August, after repeated defeats, Batista's troops had virtually withdrawn from the countryside and were surrounded in the cities. By December, members of the U.S. government who had supplied Batista with large quantities of military equipment—fearing that Castro's revolution might be taken over by the Communists—concluded that Batista could not be saved and abandoned him.

After the withdrawal of U.S. support, Batista realized that he could no longer maintain himself in power. At 2:00 A.M. on New Year's Day, 1959, he fled the country and sought asylum in the Dominican Republic. The next day, Che and the detachment of guerrillas he led entered Havana in the north, while Castro, in Santiago to the south, was making a speech before thousands of cheering Cubans. Castro announced the "popular election" of Manuel Urrutia Lleó as president of the provisional government, which would administer the country until elections could be held.

Castro began a leisurely trip to Havana, stopping often along the way to accept the admiration of throngs of Cubans. On January 8, 1959, he finally entered Havana to the thunderous cheers of hundreds of thousands of his fellow citizens. The war was over.

Chapter 6

Castro in Power

Castro had formed few plans beyond the defeat of Batista. Those who knew him at the time said he had no intention of trying to run the Cuban government himself. Some of his closest associates said Castro saw himself as the successor to one of his heroes, the great South American "Liberator," Simón Bolívar (1783-1830), and intended to lead successful revolts in other Latin American countries now that Cuba was free. He spent several months after Batista's overthrow traveling around Cuba and enjoying the adoration of the Cuban people, which manifested itself everywhere he went. Castro took the modest title Representative of the Rebel Armed Forces to the President. He left governing to the various groups that had helped him overthrow the dictatorship.

Trials and Executions

Bowing to popular pressure, the provisional government in Cuba put many members of Batista's government on trial for war crimes and atrocities against civilians. Castro himself had issued an order to his subordinates to begin the summary courts-martial of "war criminals": members of Batista's army and civilian government accused of torturing unarmed civilians and captured rebels. The trials usually resulted in convictions and executions. Castro ordered the executions to be by firing squad. One such execution was overseen by Raúl. The court tried and condemned seventy men, whose execution was recorded on film. The film was given to CBS television in the United States. The executions raised opposition in the international community, and Castro lost some of his

Fidel (left) with fellow revolutionary Che Guevara the day before their triumphant march into Havana in 1959. (AP/Wide World Photos)

popularity outside Cuba by defending the trials and verdicts. The Cuban government itself was divided over the trials—and over most other issues as well. As often happens in history, the revolutionaries realized that they could agree on little except their opposition to Batista. The immediate result was a totally ineffective government that failed to live up to the expectations of the masses.

The Cuban people and members of the provisional government virtually forced Castro to take over the responsibilities of prime minister. The members of the government had already decided that there could be no elections for at least eighteen months, so Castro received the power to rule by decree. He formulated plans to begin the sweeping reforms advocated in *History Will Absolve Me.*

Relations Abroad

Before putting his plans into action, however, Castro accepted an invitation from the Society of Newspaper Editors to attend their convention in the United States. He hoped to use the opportunity to meet high-ranking members of the U.S. government and perhaps convince the Eisenhower administration to aid Cuban development.

Castro received a hero's welcome from large crowds in New York City and Washington, D.C. In contrast, his meetings with U.S. government officials proved less than successful. The most notable of those meetings was with Vice President Richard Nixon. After the meeting, Nixon sent to the State Department a memorandum in which he argued that Castro's government threatened American interests. Nixon recommended that the Central Intelligence Agency (CIA) begin arming a rebel force to overthrow Castro. Castro developed an instant dislike for Nixon, and the rift between the two countries widened.

In the meantime, Che Guevara made an extended trip to Europe and Africa, where he held discussions with leaders of Eastern Bloc nations such as Czechoslovakia and Third World governments such as Egypt. One result of his trip was an agreement with the Czechs that they would supply Cuba with arms. Che also established contact with many Third World leaders.

After a triumphant tour of South America, where he was greeted as a conquering hero, Castro returned to Cuba determined to implement all the social reforms he had promised while leading the revolution.

"Social Justice" and Its Price

Fidel and his government benefited greatly from the general growth of the world economy that began in the late 1950's. Fidel was immensely popular with the Cuban people, and once he made the decision to run the government himself, he devoted all of his enormous energies to the task. As the economy improved, jobs became more plentiful and wages rose. Fidel's popularity increased, too—especially as he began to get rid of organized crime. However, he shrugged off questions from reporters about his relationship with the Cuban Communist Party, and he was equally evasive about holding democratic elections.

During the next two years, Castro fundamentally changed Cuban society. He established the Institute of Agrarian Reform (INRA), with himself as its president. Through the INRA, Castro redistributed agricultural land in Cuba, ensuring that all peasants had enough land from which to make a living. He divided the large estates among poor peasants and introduced modern agricultural techniques. He also initiated a national construction project designed to build modern housing for all Cubans. Castro devised a new educational system that provided free education for all children, as well as an adult

Premier Castro signs Cuba's land reform law, which will break up large land holdings and redistribute them to poor peasants. (AP/Wide World Photos)

education program to combat illiteracy. Finally, Castro
instituted a national health plan that provided adequate free
medical care for all Cubans.

These measures made Castro popular with the masses of the
Cuban people, but they came at a high price. Arguing that
society could not be changed by pluralistic democracy, Castro
established dictatorial control over the government during the
period of the reforms. To seize power from within, Castro
increasingly enlisted the aid of the Cuban Communist Party,
installing its members in key government positions. With the
full support of most Cubans, Castro delayed indefinitely the
promised parliamentary elections.

As opposition developed against Castro's policies
(especially among those whose property was distributed
among the masses), he adopted ever more repressive measures
to silence his critics. He suspended *habeas corpus* (the right to
protection against illegal imprisonment), imposed strict
censorship on the press, and created secret police to identify
"enemies of the revolution"—that is, anyone who opposed his
will.

These measures caused many members of the Cuban middle
class, especially trained technicians and professionals, to flee
the country. Many of these refugees went to the United States,
especially the Miami area in Florida. They began organizing
an anti-Castro underground and conspiring to overthrow
Castro's government. Their departure also made Castro's task
of modernizing Cuba more difficult, because those who left
were the very ones needed to build an industrialized nation.
Castro's policies also made him powerful enemies in the
United States among business owners whose property in Cuba
was nationalized. Some of these individuals, who held high
posts in the U.S. government, contributed to a process that
brought Castro to the center of the world stage and almost
resulted in nuclear war.

Chapter 7

Castro and the Cold War

Since the Spanish-American War of 1898 and the Platt Amendment of 1902-1934, many Cubans have resented what they consider the overpowering influence of the United States government in Cuban affairs. Castro shared this resentment, which in his case was made worse by U.S. support for Batista during the revolution and his own cold reception in Washington after Batista's defeat. Early in 1960, Castro began receiving reports that the Eisenhower administration was planning his overthrow, either by armed invasion or by assassination. U.S. government documents from the time—which later were declassified or obtained by journalists through the Freedom of Information Act (explored in detail by U.S. senator Frank Church in a report titled *Select Committee Report on Government Operations with Respect to Intelligence Activities and Alleged Assassination Plots Involving Foreign Leaders*, 1975)—have revealed that Castro's fears were justified.

After Castro's triumph, President Eisenhower began receiving pressure from Nixon and from the Dulles brothers, Allen and John Foster, to intervene in Cuban affairs. Allen Dulles was the head of the Central Intelligence Agency (CIA) during the Eisenhower administration; John Foster Dulles was the secretary of state. Both owned large blocks of stock in the United Fruit Company, which controlled more than 400,000 acres of agricultural land in Cuba that were eventually nationalized and redistributed to Cuban peasants. The Dulles brothers pressed Eisenhower to begin an effort to overthrow Castro. They were supported by General Robert Cutler, chairman of the National Security Council and a member of the board of directors of the United Fruit Company.

Bowing to the recommendations of these men, Eisenhower, on March 17, 1960, authorized the CIA to begin arming and training a group of Cuban exiles to invade Cuba. The project had an initial budget of $13 million. Probably unknown to the president, some members of the CIA also began planning Castro's assassination, eventually offering $150,000 plus all expenses to members of organized crime for the killing of Castro. Castro evidently became aware of this plot, because he spoke with representatives of the world press concerning the intentions of the U.S. government toward him and his regime. Eisenhower also ordered economic sanctions against Cuba.

Almost certainly these policies would have driven Castro from power had it not been for the international situation. Since 1947, the United States and the Soviet Union had been involved in an ideological struggle known as the Cold War which threatened to engulf the world in nuclear holocaust. In a desperate attempt to forestall a U.S.-led attempt to overthrow his regime in Cuba, Castro turned to the Soviet Union for aid. The resulting crisis brought the world as close as it ever came to the abyss of nuclear war.

Castro and the Soviet Union

In September, 1960, Castro traveled to New York to address the United Nations General Assembly. In one of his typical marathon speeches (this one lasted for more than four hours), he made it clear that he was determined to expose what he considered a U.S. plot to overthrow his government. After his speech, Fidel was upstaged one of the few times in his life when the bald, chubby leader of the Soviet Union, Nikita Khrushchev, took off one of his shoes and pounded the table with it to show his displeasure when the U.S. spokesman attempted to deny Castro's charges. According to his aides,

Fidel Castro and Soviet Premier Nikita Khrushchev shake hands in Moscow after a Soviet-Cuban agreement. (AP/Wide World Photos)

Khrushchev had come to the United Nations determined to draw Castro into the bloc of Soviet nations, even though high-ranking Soviet officials thought Khrushchev's plan was too risky.

By this time, Castro had concluded that his government could survive only with the help of a powerful ally that could shore up the now-sagging Cuban economy and provide military protection from the anticipated U.S. invasion of the island. He was therefore more than receptive to Khrushchev's overtures of friendship. Some of Castro's advisers have since written that he was aware that he might be trading U.S. domination for Soviet domination. He also realized that his actions could provoke a war between the superpowers. Castro was willing to take those risks, which involved literally billions of lives, in the hope of securing independence for Cuba.

Despite skepticism concerning Castro among other Soviet leaders, Khrushchev began a process that eventually guaranteed markets for Cuban products in Soviet Bloc nations and provided long-term credits for the modernization of the Cuban economy. Within a short time, the Soviet Union also began providing military assistance to Cuba, which included large quantities of military equipment and the stationing of Soviet military personnel on Cuban soil. For Castro, this new relationship with the Soviet Union seemed to solve all his pressing economic and security problems. For Khrushchev, it seemed a major victory in the Cold War. For the United States government, it seemed totally unacceptable.

U.S.-Cuban relations deteriorated completely after Castro's agreement with the Soviet Union. In October, Eisenhower ordered a complete stoppage of U.S. exports to Cuba (called an *embargo*), with the exception of medical supplies. Castro responded by nationalizing most remaining U.S.-owned businesses and banks in Cuba. Eisenhower then ended Cuban sugar sales in the U.S. market and withdrew the U.S. ambassador to Cuba. War seemed inevitable.

The Bay of Pigs Invasion

During the 1960 U.S. presidential election campaign, the Democratic candidate, John F. Kennedy, called for the U.S.-led organization of a Cuban exile force to overthrow Castro. He was unaware that such a plan was already well advanced. In a reply, Richard Nixon, the Republican candidate, called Kennedy's statement "shockingly irresponsible." Castro, convinced that the Eisenhower administration would launch an invasion before going out of office, ordered a general mobilization of all Cuban forces. However, Eisenhower left office before the plan went into effect.

After Kennedy's inauguration in March, 1961, the new president found that he had inherited a plan for an invasion of Cuba that involved active participation by U.S. combat forces. Kennedy ultimately proved unwilling to commit U.S. troops to the project, which resulted in one of the greatest embarrassments of his administration.

Kennedy's advisers could not agree on whether or not to pursue the CIA invasion plan when they learned of it. Kennedy finally opted to go ahead with the plan, but at the last moment he refused to order the U.S. Air Force to supply air support for the invasion. This refusal may have been based on an inaccurate intelligence report indicating that Castro's air force had already been destroyed in an attack by his own Cuban enemies.

Without the expected air support, the invasion was a total failure. With Castro in personal command of the Cuban army, his men killed or captured most of the invaders shortly after they landed in Cuba at the Bay of Pigs on April 15, 1961. Friends and relatives of the invaders blamed the U.S. government and especially Kennedy for the deaths of their loved ones. The failed invasion had the ultimate effect of uniting the Cuban people more firmly than ever behind their leader. Castro had successfully defied the most powerful nation in the world.

Cuba Goes Communist

Kennedy later abandoned plans for an invasion of Cuba, choosing instead to isolate the island from its trading partners in the Western Hemisphere. Before the Bay of Pigs fiasco, Kennedy had announced a plan for Latin American modernization that he called the Alliance for Progress. The Alliance evolved into an organ for distributing U.S. loans and grants to any Latin American government that would join the United States in an economic boycott of Cuba.

Most Latin American governments joined the Alliance for Progress. In response, Castro declared Cuba a "socialist" state, canceled the scheduled elections, and elevated more members of the Cuban Communist Party to high positions in his government. Denied markets for Cuban goods in the Western Hemisphere, Castro also formed trade agreements with Soviet Bloc countries. Cuba was now in a very close relationship with the Soviet Union. In December, 1961, Castro announced formally that he was himself a Marxist-Leninist. Essentially, Cuba had become a Communist country.

The Cuban Missile Crisis

With Castro firmly in the Soviet camp, Khrushchev decided in early 1962 to secure a foothold in the Western Hemisphere by increasing the Soviets' military presence in Cuba. In April, the Soviet Union began preparations to deploy missiles in Cuba. These missiles were capable of hitting targets anywhere in the United States and could carry nuclear warheads. Castro agreed to accept these weapons, along with the twenty thousand Soviet military personnel necessary to operate them. He thought that the Soviet presence would deter any further U.S. invasion plans.

On August 23, 1962, John McCone, the new director of the CIA, informed President Kennedy that the Soviet military was installing offensive weapons in Cuba. Rumors concerning the missiles began emerging in U.S. newspapers, magazines, and television broadcasts shortly thereafter, provoking an outcry of anti-Cuban opinion from the American public. On October 14,

U.S. spy planes flying over Cuba produced evidence that confirmed McCone's report to the president. Photographs taken by U-2 aircraft over the next six days showed clearly that the installation of sites for the missiles was nearly completed.

U.S. President John F. Kennedy addresses the American people on the eve of the Cuban Missile Crisis. (AP/Wide World Photos)

On October 22, Kennedy went on national television to inform the American people and the world that he was ordering a "quarantine" of Cuba. U.S. armed forces would encircle Cuba to enforce the quarantine, barring any offensive military equipment from being sent to the island. Khrushchev replied that he would not be deterred by U.S. "blackmail" and ordered Soviet ships to deliver the missiles to Cuba. Neither Kennedy nor Khrushchev consulted Castro during this tense period, which infuriated him. Castro believed that he had been reduced to the status of a mere pawn in the world chess game of the Cold War.

For the next six days, the world came perilously close to nuclear war. Soviet ships sailed toward the cordon of American warships surrounding Cuba. The American ships were under orders not to let the Soviets pass. American television networks broadcast the dramatic events of the crisis live across the nation. At the last moment, the U.S. and Soviet leaders struck a bargain and the Soviet ships turned back.

Castro's New Stance

Castro felt that he had been betrayed by Khrushchev and vowed never again to let himself be used in the global struggle between the superpowers. Kennedy and Khrushchev had agreed to guarantee Cuba's national security, but that did not lessen Castro's sense of betrayal. Castro began a campaign to establish himself as the leader of the "non-aligned nations": those Third World nations that pursued a course independent of the superpowers of the Cold War. The publicity and notoriety that Castro gained during his successful defiance of the United States aided him greatly in his new quest.

Chapter 8

Voice of the Third World

For two years after the Cuban Missile Crisis, Castro concentrated on domestic affairs, trying to modernize his nation and raise the standard of living for his people. He used the Soviet example as his model. Events in the United States and the Soviet Union, however, catapulted Castro once again into the center of world affairs.

In 1963, President Kennedy fell to an assassin's bullet. His successor, Lyndon Baines Johnson, became so heavily involved in the escalating war in Vietnam that he and his advisers began paying less attention to affairs in the Third World.

Early the next year, Khrushchev fell from power in the Soviet Union. His successors proved unwilling to become involved in Third World liberation movements after their humiliation in Cuba, leaving a vacuum in international affairs. These events allowed Castro to assume a growing role in what came to be called the Non-Aligned Movement.

Castro and World Revolution

Propagandists in the United States had long accused Castro of fomenting violent revolts throughout Latin America. Prior to 1964, those charges were largely untrue. In 1964, Castro (at the urging of his revolutionary comrade Che Guevara) decided to do exactly what the U.S. government and press had accused him of doing. With the approval of officials in the Soviet Union, he began sending Cuban troops, advisers on guerrilla warfare, and military supplies to revolutionary groups in several Latin American and African countries that were

Shortly after his own victory in Cuba, Castro arrives in Venezuela to celebrate that nation's overthrow of dictator Marcos Perez. (AP/Wide World Photos)

revolting against what they perceived as corrupt governments controlled by European and American imperialists.

Che led the Cuban move into the international revolutionary arena. He toured Africa in late 1964 and established a number of contacts that he hoped to organize into a continent-wide revolutionary movement. Che persuaded Castro to send military aid to several of the African revolutionary groups, especially to Alphonse Massamba-Débat in the Congo. Che himself led a band of 125 guerrillas in the struggle in central Africa, adopting tactics very similar to those that had brought Castro to power in Cuba. As a result of his championing of Third World revolution, Castro began to emerge as the leader of the Non-Aligned Movement.

The groups Castro supported in Africa were not successful, mainly because there was no unity in the revolutionary movement there. Nevertheless, Castro's reputation continued to grow, because everywhere he sent Cuban troops, he also sent doctors, agricultural experts, and teachers to raise the standard of living of the people. In 1965, he sent to the Congo an additional seven hundred Cuban troops, who helped Massamba-Débat establish a socialist republic there.

The funds and resources necessary to pursue this aggressive foreign policy placed a tremendous strain on the Cuban economy. Despite his commitment to Third World wars of liberation, Castro curtailed his foreign ventures for almost a decade after 1965 in order to concentrate on building Cuba into a modern industrialized nation. He did, however, continue to finance a guerrilla warfare training base in Africa and to maintain several thousand Cuban military advisers abroad. Although he devoted fewer Cuban resources to Third World revolutions, his stature and reputation as the leading figure of the Non-Aligned Movement continued to grow because of his diplomatic activities.

The Tricontinental Congress

In January, 1966, Havana hosted the first Tricontinental Congress of Non-Aligned Nations. In his opening address before the delegates from most Third World countries, Castro proclaimed that Cuba would aid any revolutionary movement that was fighting against imperialism. The statement provoked prolonged applause from the delegates, who began looking to Castro, not to the Soviet Union, for help in their struggle against foreign domination.

The next year, 1967, Castro created the Latin American Solidarity Organization (OLAS) and convened its first meeting in Havana. Castro invited representatives from all the revolutionary movements in the various Latin American states and promised them help to fight against "American imperialism." The meeting established Castro as the unquestioned leader of the revolutionary groups, but it damaged any hope for an improvement in U.S.-Cuban relations.

Castro's promises were largely empty. The Cuban economic situation did not permit large-scale aid to anyone. Castro tried desperately during the late 1960's to modernize Cuba. He set forth a plan for the country to produce 10 million tons of sugar in 1970. The profits from this huge crop would be used to buy modern industrial equipment. Castro mobilized the entire nation to meet this unrealistic goal. He himself worked in the sugarcane fields. Billboards and television broadcasts asked Cuban citizens the question, "What are you doing toward the 10 million?" Cubans toiled but were able to produce only 8 million tons of sugar for the year—a stunning achievement, but short of the goal. In another effort to achieve economic growth, Castro joined COMECON (a common market composed of many nations from the Soviet Bloc), but still the Cuban economy did not provide enough surplus for Castro to send substantial quantities of supplies to other countries.

Without the massive aid promised by Castro, Latin American liberation movements began to collapse, and few of them survived the 1960's. The defeat of a group led by Che Guevara in Bolivia in 1967 and Che's later execution caused Castro great personal anguish.

Guevara, disillusioned with the direction of the Cuban revolution, tried to implement the same tactics he and Castro had used successfully in Cuba to overthrow the Bolivian government. He and his small group of followers were never able to attract a large number of followers or sympathizers among the Bolivian people. Bolivian soldiers tracked him down and, after capturing him, shot him without a trial.

After the events in Bolivia, Cuban-inspired movements in Venezuela, Guatemala, and Colombia soon collapsed. By the early 1970's, even Castro acknowledged that armed revolution had failed in Latin America.

U. S. Secretary of State Henry Kissinger. (Library of Congress)

Castro and Kissinger

Castro's decision to join COMECON resulted in another confrontation with the United States. This time, however, it almost resulted in the United States and Cuba becoming friends. With Cuba's participation in COMECON, Soviet officials suspended all interest payments on the $4 billion that Cuba owed to the Soviet Union for loans, and all payments on the principal until 1986 (in 1986, the payments on interest were further postponed until 1999). This agreement provided relief for Castro's struggling economy and permitted Castro to continue to devote much of his nation's income to social programs. In return, the Soviets required that the Soviet navy be allowed to build submarine bases in Cuba. Castro and Soviet leader Leonid Brezhnev may have believed that President Richard Nixon's administration was too distracted by the nightmarish war in Vietnam to risk another confrontation over Cuba. If that was their belief, they were mistaken.

When U.S. intelligence agencies reported to Nixon that the Soviets were building submarine bases, Nixon's secretary of state, Henry Kissinger, immediately informed the Soviets that such bases would not be tolerated by the United States. Soviet officials quickly complied with Kissinger's demands that the bases be dismantled.

The foreign policy of the United States under the direction of Nixon and Kissinger aimed at *détente* (the establishment of friendly relations) with the Communist world. In pursuing this policy, Nixon granted formal U.S. diplomatic recognition to Communist "Red" China (the People's Republic of China), began arms-reduction negotiations with the Soviets, and made other attempts to lessen the tensions of the Cold War. After the submarine crisis, Kissinger also made friendly overtures to Cuba. Representatives of the two nations began talks aimed at settling all the outstanding differences between the United

States and Cuba. One immediate result of these negotiations was a vote by the Organization of American States (OAS) to lift all economic barriers against Cuba. Also, the Latin American countries that were members of the OAS decided to grant diplomatic recognition to Castro's government. However, just when the talks seemed certain to be successful, events in Africa drove a new wedge between Castro and the United States.

In the spring of 1975, Castro sent large numbers of Cuban troops to Angola—a nation on the southwest coast of Africa—to fight against U.S.-backed forces there. U.S. officials warned Castro to cease his interference in Angola or else they would break off the talks for normalized diplomatic relations with Cuba. Castro insisted on his right to conduct Cuban foreign policy without the United States telling him what to do; he continued to increase the Cuban military presence in Angola. In return, U.S. negotiators dropped their efforts to come to an understanding with Castro.

The Non-Aligned Movement

Castro's support of Angolan independence immediately reestablished him as the most important leader of the growing Non-Aligned Movement. Cuban successes against the combined forces of U.S.- and Soviet-backed guerrilla fighters and the regular South African army won Castro the praise of Third World nations, and a new wave of patriotic pride swept over Cuba. Cubans were almost as proud of their small nation's renewed ability to stand up to the "bully" of Western imperialism as they had been after the Bay of Pigs crisis more than a decade earlier. Castro was once again a hero at home and abroad.

The Non-Aligned Summit opened in Havana in the immediate aftermath of Cuban-supported revolutionary movements in Grenada and Nicaragua. However, rather than

89

sounding a battle cry for world revolution, Castro adopted a new approach to obtain justice for Third World peoples: a humanitarian call for men and women everywhere to join in a common struggle to create a better world.

Addressing the U.N. General Assembly one month after the Havana summit, Castro again appealed to the collective conscience of the people of the industrialized world. Only the collective efforts of all humankind, Castro said, could solve the massive suffering of human beings around the globe who did not have food to eat, schools to educate them, or doctors to heal them. The Cuban leader's words were persuasive even to many of his former enemies. The U.N. speech was Castro's finest hour.

Chapter 9

Castro's Legacy

When historians write about Fidel Castro one hundred years from now, they will certainly conclude that he profoundly influenced the course of world history during his era. Critics will point out that many of his actions were detrimental to the purposes he espoused. Supporters will note that he had a positive influence in his own country and in Third World nations abroad. All, however, must agree that for the leader of a tiny country to have played such a large role in international affairs was remarkable and required a unique individual.

Castro's Legacy to Cuba

Castro's economic and social legacy to Cuba is mixed. He has taken credit for much-publicized gains in areas such as health care, education, housing, and transportation. To some degree, his claims are justified, but the statistics he cites to support them are misleading. In many cases, the improvements are the result of trends that began before 1959 and had little to do with the revolution. For example, Castro boasts that he has eliminated diseases such as measles and polio from his island. Fidel is only partially justified in his claim: He has made basic medical care, such as inoculations against many diseases, available to all Cubans; however, the elimination of those diseases resulted from medical technology developed outside Cuba.

Castro claims that the revolution has provided modern housing for all its citizens, complete with sanitary facilities unknown outside urban areas of the island before 1959. Housing was high on Fidel's list of projects immediately after the revolution, and his programs made impressive strides during the first few years. His many foreign projects have since drained the national budget of needed revenue to the point that few new housing units are being built to shelter a growing population. The result is growing numbers of slums around urban areas.

Fidel also claims to have created greater social mobility in Cuba, enabling people from the lower classes to rise to high positions and high wages through hard work. In reality, most of the high positions in government and industry are already filled and few new jobs are being created, making it very difficult for members of the younger generation—no matter how well educated—to succeed.

Castro's government has created one of the best education systems in the world, but even this may prove unhappy for Castro in the long run. Cuba has experienced a population explosion since 1959, its people increasing from about 6.5 million to more than 10 million. More than 50 percent of Cubans alive in 1992 were born after the revolution and thus know little about Fulgencio Batista or the corruption of Cuban government before Castro. The young people of this new generation seem increasingly impatient with Castro's promises of a better life in the future and disillusioned with the lack of opportunities in Cuba. More than a million of these young people have emigrated from Cuba since 1959, and many of those who remain in Cuba are secretly critical of Castro, according to interviews reported by some American journalists. These young people, according to the interviews, look forward to the death of the aging dictator so that a new day can dawn for Cuba.

What social mobility has existed under Castro has not been extended to women and minorities. Most members of the large African population of Cuba still occupy the lowest rungs of the socioeconomic ladder. Women, although equal with men according to the law, still suffer economic and political discrimination.

In a summary of Castro's economic and social policies, one economist has written that the most significant effect of Castro's policies has been to eliminate the most privileged sectors of society and to raise up the poor. As a result, the worst examples of poverty have disappeared, but the living standard of other citizens has gone down. Instead of shared wealth, Castro has created shared poverty; goods are rationed and there seems to be a shortage of almost everything.

Castro's legacy in the area of human rights is also open to question. In 1975, Castro established a new constitution for Cuba concurrently with the convention of the first official Communist Party Congress. The constitution merged the offices of prime minister and president in the person of Fidel Castro, making him the unquestioned dictator of the nation in name as well as in fact. The constitution prohibits political organizations other than the Communist Party, which means no representative government. Castro rationalizes the lack of democracy by insisting that he and he alone knows the will of the Cuban people, and therefore parliamentary debates are not necessary.

Cubans may criticize the actions of individual ministries within the government, but Castro's secret police (aided by a large network of informers) arrest and imprison anyone who criticizes Castro or the tenets of Marxism-Leninism. For most of Castro's long tenure as dictator, Cuba has had more political prisoners than any other nation in the world. Castro has steadfastly refused to let humanitarian organizations such as Amnesty International investigate the conditions of his prisons. This situation changed only when Castro tried to empty his prisons and insane asylums during the Mariel boat lift, perhaps the most embarrassing incident of Castro's career.

The "Boat People"

Early in 1980, many Cubans gathered near the unguarded
Peruvian embassy in Havana, claiming political asylum.
Castro tried to get the refugees out of sight by allowing those
who wished to leave to depart for the United States from the
nearby port of Mariel. As more people learned that they were
free to emigrate, huge numbers of them flocked to Mariel,

*U.S. Marines lift a Cuban child off one of the boats carrying Cuban refugees from Mariel
to Florida in 1980.* (AP/Wide World Photos)

from which a large fleet of private boats transported more than
one hundred thousand of them to the United States. Castro,
humiliated at this demonstration that his regime was not
universally popular with the Cuban people, freed most political
prisoners (and common criminals) and most insane asylum
inmates and sent them to the United States with the refugees.

Officials in the United States could not accommodate all the

Cubans who wanted to come to America, so they persuaded Castro during secret negotiations to halt the process at his end. More than two thousand Cubans who came to the United States in the Mariel boat lift would remain imprisoned in a federal facility in Atlanta, Georgia, without being charged with a crime or given a trial. As a result of the bad feelings on both sides, another round of talks between the United States and Cuba collapsed.

The Mariel incident demonstrates that Castro had not eliminated dissent in Cuba, but merely suppressed it. Although the constitution of 1975 guarantees all Cubans freedom of speech, press, and religion, in reality the citizens of Castro's island enjoy none of those cherished human rights. In the schools and universities teachers may say whatever they like—so long as their lectures do not conflict with Marxist-Leninist dogma. Even a casual remark on the street critical of Castro or the socialist system may be overheard by the large network of informers and result in arrest and imprisonment for the unwary person who uttered it. Castro himself professes adherence to Christianity, but his actions toward organized religion in Cuba suggest that it will be tolerated only so long as it does not teach doctrine that conflicts with what Castro thinks is in the best interests of the state.

Since 1985, Castro has suffered a number of embarrassments and setbacks that make the future of his revolution uncertain. Revelations that high-ranking members of his government have been involved in the international drug trade and other criminal activities make it increasingly difficult to distinguish between Fidel's regime and the corrupt dictatorships that preceded it. Fidel was further embarrassed in 1991 when many working-class Cubans fled his island for Florida, some of them on inner-tubes, in an effort to escape the stagnant Cuban economy.

Castro's Legacy to the World

Like his legacy to the Cuban people, Castro has left to the world community a curious mixture of positive achievements and doctrines destructive to the causes he claims to champion. Castro's demands for justice for the people of the Third World have touched the consciences of the people and the diplomats of the industrialized countries. He has presented the delegates to the United Nations General Assembly with constant demands that the developed nations of the world provide aid to the people of poorer regions. Castro's demands have been instrumental in the establishment of the many U.N. agencies designed to distribute food, medicine, and knowledge to poor people in Africa, Asia, and Latin America. He has also provided leadership in the growing global awareness of environmental problems.

On the debit side of Castro's international ledger must be included his support of bloody rebellions in order to gain the political and economic ends he deems desirable. Castro has freely given his blessing to guerrilla movements around the globe, including terrorist groups. Castro's advocacy of such groups has contributed to the deaths of hundreds of thousands of men, women, and children—usually members of the poorest classes in society, the people he says he represents.

Castro has also shown some of the hypocrisy that seems to plague all politicians. He speaks eloquently before international audiences about human rights but suppresses human rights in Cuba. He violently denounced the actions of the United States in Vietnam and Grenada, but he refused to condemn the Soviet Union for its invasion of Afghanistan during the 1980's. That failure cost him much credibility and support among Third World nations. Castro talks about the industrialized nations' responsibility to save the global environment, but he is unwilling to adopt "green" policies in Cuba. Although this lack of consistency is far from unique

96

among politicians anywhere, it nevertheless makes Castro less appealing to many people around the world.

A book by Cuban novelist José Lezama Lima, previously banned by the Cuban government, again became available in 1991. Here, crowds of Cubans clamor to buy it. (Lou DeMatteis)

Castro in Retrospect

Generations to come in Cuba may venerate Castro as the man who brought something approaching social and economic equality to the Cuban people. They may also despise him for having suppressed basic human freedoms without which the quality of life is greatly diminished. Whether future historians depict Castro as a hero or a scoundrel—or, more likely, something in between—will depend on how they balance his tyranny with his humanitarianism.

Biographers in the future will have an equally difficult time agreeing on Castro's influence on the world community. Many will undoubtedly applaud his championing of the underprivileged people of the world, his advocacy of environmentalism, and his courage in leading a tiny nation in successful opposition to the superpowers. Others will certainly condemn him for supporting violent revolutions that led to enormous bloodshed. All of those biographers, however, will agree on one point: Fidel Castro left an indelible imprint on the history of his era.

Major Achievements

Achievement	Date	Significance
Cuban Revolution	1956-1959	First true attempt to bring democracy and socioeconomic equality to Cuba
Land reform	1961	Creates INRA, an agency that redistributes agricultural land in Cuba, ensuring that all peasants have enough land to make a living
Educational reform	1962	Provides all Cuban children with access to education to the limits of their ability
Health care reform	1962	Makes basic health care available to all Cubans
Housing reform	1962	Builds modern, sanitary housing for all citizens
Non-Aligned Movement	1966-1979	Provides a voice in world affairs for the small and poor nations of the world

Time Line

1927	*August 13.* Fidel Alejandro Castro Ruz is born in Oriente Province, Cuba.
1945	*September.* Castro matriculates at the University of Havana.
1948	*October 12.* Marries Mirta Díaz-Balart.
1950	*June.* Receives his doctorates in law and social science.
1952	*February.* Announces his candidacy for the Cuban parliament on the *Ortodoxo* ticket.
1952	*March 10.* Fulgencio Batista overthrows the Cuban government and cancels scheduled elections, declaring himself president. Castro becomes convinced that only revolution can end corruption in Cuba.
1952	*May.* Castro organizes a movement to overthrow Batista. He begins writing revolutionary articles under the pseudonym Alejandro for the underground newspaper El Acusador (The Accuser).
1953	*July 26.* Castro and his supporters attempt to take over the Moncada military barracks in Oriente Province; they hope to incite a general revolution. The attack is unsuccessful; Castro and other survivors are captured two days later.
1953	*September.* Castro and his co-conspirators undergo trial for treason. Castro uses trial as forum to denounce Batista and justify his own actions. His closing statement, widely circulated as a booklet entitled *History Will Absolve Me* becomes the inspiration for the Cuban revolution. He is sentenced to fifteen years in prison on the Isle of Pines.
1955	*May-July.* Batista frees all political prisoners, including Castro and his supporters. Castro forms the July 26 Movement, a secret revolutionary organization, and goes into exile in Mexico. There he meets Che Guevara and they plan the revolution.
1956	*December 2.* Castro and eighty-one followers aboard the yacht *Granma* land in Cuba near Belic in Oriente Province. The revolution begins.
1959	*January 1.* Batista flees Cuba.

100

1959	*January 8*. Castro triumphantly enters Havana, taking the title Representative of the Rebel Armed Forces to the President.
1959	*February*. Castro becomes prime minister.
1959	*April-May*. Castro is welcomed as a hero during a tour of Latin America.
1959	*May 17*. Castro begins redistribution of agricultural lands in Cuba.
1959-1960	Castro suspends *habeas corpus*, creates secret police to eliminate "enemies of the revolution," and ends freedom of the press in Cuba.
1960	*February*. Castro signs a major trade agreement between Cuba and the Soviet Union.
1960	*March*. President Eisenhower authorizes the CIA to begin arming and training a group of Cuban exiles to invade Cuba.
1960	*May*. Castro begins socialization of the Cuban economy. He sends arms and medical supplies to revolutionaries in Algeria to show Cuban support for the struggle against imperialism.
1960	*September*. The CIA contracts with members of U.S. Mafia for Castro's assassination. Khrushchev agrees to give Cuba military aid to help repulse the anticipated U.S. invasion of Cuba.
1961	*January*. Diplomatic relations between the United States and Cuba cease.
1961	*April 17*. The Bay of Pigs invasion is repulsed.
1961	*May 1*. Castro suspends all elections in Cuba.
1961	*December*. Castro proclaims himself a Marxist-Leninist.
1962	*January*. Cuba is expelled from the Organization of American States.
1962	*May*. The Soviet Union begins supplying Cuba with large quantities of military equipment and building facilities for ballistic missiles in Cuba.
1962	*October 22*. The Cuban Missile Crisis brings the United States and the Soviet Union to the brink of nuclear war.

1965	Castro sends seven hundred military advisers, along with teachers, doctors, and agricultural experts, to aid revolutionaries in the Congo. This marks the beginning of large-scale Cuban support for anti-imperialist wars of liberation around the world.
1966	*January 3*. Cuba hosts the Tricontinental Congress of representatives from Third World countries.
1967	*August*. Castro creates the Latin American Solidarity Organization, designed to spearhead revolutionary activity in Western Hemisphere.
1967	*October 9*. Che is executed in Bolivia. Other Cuban-supported movements in Latin America are destroyed at about the same time.
1972	*July*. Cuba joins COMECON.
1972	*December*. Several Latin American states defy the United States and reestablish relations with Cuba.
1975	Castro sends troops to aid the revolutionary movement in Angola.
	The Organization of American States votes to lift all sanctions against Cuba.
	The first Cuban Communist Party Congress convenes.
	A new Cuban constitution is promulgated, proclaiming Castro to be both prime minister and president of Cuba.
1976	Angolan rebels, supported by Cuban troops, triumph over rival factions supported by the United States, South Africa, and Israel.
1979	Castro becomes chairman of an organization of Third World governments.
	The Sandinista revolution in Nicaragua and the New Jewel movement in Grenada succeed.
1980	*Summer*. Mariel boat lift.
Late 1980's	High-ranking members of Castro's government begin illegal drug dealing. Eventually caught, their trials and executions greatly embarrass Castro.
1991	Poor Cubans flee to Florida on inner-tubes to escape Cuba's poor economic conditions.

Glossary

Alliance for Progress: A U.S.-sponsored agreement between governments in the Western Hemisphere to cooperate in modernization and resisting Communism. Signed in 1962, one of its purposes was to minimize trade between Cuba and other American states.

Angola: A nation on the western coast of Africa into which Castro sent large numbers of Cuban troops to aid rebels in a struggle to throw off European domination.

Annexation: The incorporation of a territory into the domain of another nation.

*Auténticos***:** The Authentic Revolutionary Movement. One of three major political parties in Cuba at the beginning of Castro's revolution. Led by Ramón Grau San Martín, the party represented itself as the opponent of corruption.

Bay of Pigs: One of two sites where the ill-fated U.S.-backed rebels landed in April of 1961, with the intent of overthrowing Castro. The beach is located on the southern coast of Cuba, approximately 110 miles southeast of Havana.

Charisma: A special, magnetic charm or appeal.

Cold War: A conflict between nations carried on by methods other than warfare.

Communism: A system of government in which a single political party controls the state-owned means of production and the distribution of goods.

*Coup d'état***:** The violent overthrow of a government by a small group of people.

Democracy: A political system in which all citizens are allowed to vote for representatives who make up the government.

Emancipation: The freeing of slaves.

Embargo: The decision of one nation to cut off all trade with another nation.

*Granma***:** The name of the boat on which Castro and his men landed in Cuba to begin their revolution, and later the name of the only newspaper permitted in Cuba, which airs Castro's personal views.

Guerrilla: A soldier who fights from ambush as a member of a small group rather than as a part of a large army.

*Habeas corpus***:** The right to be charged with a crime after arrest.

Imperialism: The domination and economic exploitation of an area of one country by another.

Insurrection: A wide-scale, violent uprising of a population against its government.

Insurrectionary: A person who promotes or takes part in an insurrection.

July 26 Movement: The name for Castro's underground revolutionary movement, which eventually swept him into power.

Land reform: The redistribution of land, usually from those who own much land to those who own little or none.

Martyr: A person who sacrifices his or her life for a cause.

Moncada: The site of an army installation that Castro and a few followers unsuccessfully attacked in 1953. Located in Oriente Province, it became the symbol of the revolutionary movement.

Non-aligned nations: The nations of the world that try to conduct their own affairs without close relations with a superpower nation.

Organization of American States: A U.S.-dominated body designed to provide a forum on which representatives of the governments of all nations in the Western Hemisphere may air grievances and settle disputes.

***Ortodoxos*:** An informal name for the Party of the Cuban People. One of three major political parties in Cuba at the beginning of Castro's revolution. Castro joined the party during his student years because he admired the party's leader, Eduardo Chibás, and its program, which called for liberal reforms and an end to foreign domination of Cuba.

Parliamentary system of government: A system of government with elected representatives who make laws and govern their nation.

Platt Amendment: A U.S. congressional act, passed in 1902, which basically claimed for the United States the right to control Cuban affairs. The act was passed in the wake of the Spanish-American War and laid down the conditions under which the United States would withdraw its troops. Cuba was not allowed to transfer land to any nation other than the United States, and the United States was allowed to intervene in Cuba's affairs "for the preservation of Cuban independence."

Provisional government: A government of appointed officials who rule until a permanent government takes office.

Regime: The whole range of government officials and agencies, usually under a head of state.

Repression: The prevention by force of normal expression, activity, and development.

Revolutionary: A person who advocates a quick and drastic change in one or more of the basic institutions of a government or society.

Socialism: An economic system in which all the people collectively own the means of production, such as factories, land, and buildings.

Third World nations: The undeveloped countries of the world, including many Latin American and African nations, populated by large numbers of poor people.

Bibliography

Bourne, Peter G. *Fidel: A Biography of Fidel Castro.* New York: Dodd, Mead & Co., 1986. A fairly objective and complete account of Castro's life and career.

Callen, Monte H. *Analysis of the Military Strategies and Warfare Principles of Che Guevara and Fidel Castro During the Cuban Revolution.* Maxwell Air Force Base, Ala.: Air Command and Staff College, 1985. A detailed and advanced analysis of the methods that brought Castro military victory against Fulgencio Batista. For those wishing to understand the military aspects of Castro's revolution.

Church, Frank. *Select Committee Report on Government Operations with Respect to Intelligence Activities and Alleged Assassination Plots Involving Foreign Leaders.* Senate Report 94-465, November 20, 1975. Washington, D.C.: Government Printing Office, 1975. A dry but comprehensive account of various U.S. government plans to assassinate Castro.

Hachey, Thomas E., and Ralph E. Weber, eds. *The Awakening of a Sleeping Giant: Third World Leaders and National Liberation.* Huntington, N.Y.: R. E. Krieger, 1981. Discusses the Third World movement and explains why Castro is its most important leader.

Halperin, Maurice. *The Rise and Decline of Fidel Castro: An Essay in Contemporary History.* Berkeley: University of California Press, 1972. An unsympathetic account of Castro's life and career and a prediction of his ouster from power.

Martin, Lionel. *The Young Fidel.* Secaucus, N.J.: Lyle Stuart, 1983. An informal account, accessible to younger readers, concerning Castro's career to 1959. Contains more information concerning Castro's childhood and school career than is available in most other sources.

Matthews, Herbert Lionel. *Fidel Castro.* New York: Simon & Schuster, 1969. A readable older biography of Castro, depicting him as a political opportunist and a willing dupe of the Soviet Union.

Oppenheimer, Andres. *Castro's Final Hour: The Secret Story Behind the Coming Downfall of Communist Cuba.* New York: Simon & Schuster, 1992. Exposes the corruption that has infiltrated Castro's regime. Argues that the generation of Cubans born since the revolution will not allow communism to survive Fidel.

Robbins, Carla Anne. *The Cuban Threat.* New York: McGraw-Hill, 1983.

The best account available concerning the Third World movement and the importance of Castro in that movement.

Szulc, Tad. *Fidel: A Critical Portrait*. New York: William Morrow, 1986. A comprehensive biography of Castro.

Thomas, Hugh. *Cuba: The Pursuit of Freedom*. New York: Harper & Row, 1971. Places Castro and his revolution in the larger context of Cuban history. Best work in English for explaining the social conditions that brought Castro to power and made him so popular with the Cuban people.

_____. *The Cuban Revolution*. New York: Harper & Row, 1977. The best and most objective account of Castro's revolution.

Media Resources

In Our Time: Cuban Premier Fidel Castro. Filmstrip and cassette, 35 minutes. 1985. Distributed by Random House. A superficial but enjoyable overview of Castro and contemporary Cuba.

Phil Donahue Show. Video, 30 minutes. New York: ABC, 1985. Interview with Michael Drosin concerning his book entitled *Citizen Huges,* in which he discusses the plans of President Kennedy and the CIA to use Mafia hit men to assassinate Castro.

Spokesmen of the Third World. Recording, 21 minutes. 1979. Distributed by Encyclopedia Americana. Castro speaks in one of a series of ten cassettes concerning the problems of the Third World and the measures that developed nations such as the United States should take to aid poorer nations of the world to create decent standards of living for their people.

Visnews, producer. *Fidel Castro.* Audiovisual, 25 minutes. Princeton, N.J.: Films for the Humanities & Sciences, 1990. A brief overview of the life and career of Castro and an assessment of his place among modern world leaders. Designed for young audiences.

Wolper, David L., producer. *Fidel Castro.* Audiovisual, 26 minutes. Los Angeles: McGraw-Hill Text-Films, 1969. One of McGraw-Hill's Biography series audiovisuals, designed for young adult audiences. An older but not inaccurate videotape.

Wolper, David L., producer. *Nikita Khrushchev, Fidel Castro, Mao Tse-tung.* Audiovisual, 60 minutes. Norwalk, Conn.: Easton Press Video, 1988. A comparison of the careers of three Marxist leaders and their influence on one another and on the world. Designed for young adult audiences.

INDEX